1947 U.S.

YEARBOOK

ISBN-10: 1539744957
ISBN-13: 978-1539744955

INDEX

	Page
People In High Office	4
Events	8
Births - U.S. Personalities	14
Popular Music	19
Top 5 Films	25
Sporting Winners	41
Cost Of Living	51

FIRST EDITION

PEOPLE IN HIGH OFFICE

President: Harry S. Truman
Democratic Party: April 12, 1945 - January 20, 1953

Born May 8, 1884, Truman served as the 33rd President of the United States succeeding to the presidency on April 12, 1945 when Roosevelt died after months of declining health. Harry S. Truman died December 26, 1972.

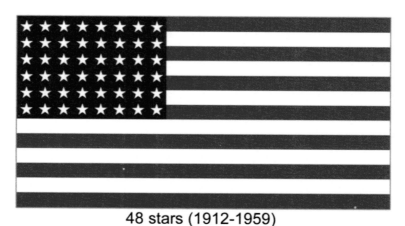

48 stars (1912-1959)

Vice President: (*Vacant 1945-1949*)
Chief Justice: Fred M. Vinson
Speaker of the House of Representatives: Joseph William Martin, Jr.
Senate Majority Leader: Wallace H. White, Jr.

United Kingdom

Prime Minister
Clement Attlee - Labour Party
July 26, 1945 - October 26, 1951

Monarch: George VI

Rest Of The World

Australia

Prime Minister
Ben Chifley

Brazil

President
Eurico Gaspar Dutra

Canada

Prime Minister
William Lyon Mackenzie King

Republic Of
China

Premiers
Soong Tse-ven
Chiang Kai-shek
Chang Ch'ün

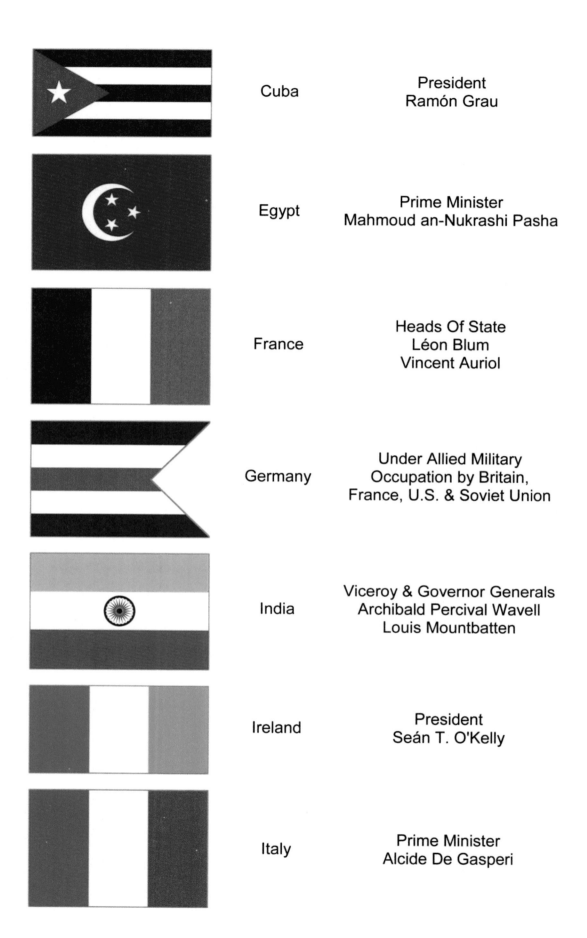

Cuba — President Ramón Grau

Egypt — Prime Minister Mahmoud an-Nukrashi Pasha

France — Heads Of State Léon Blum Vincent Auriol

Germany — Under Allied Military Occupation by Britain, France, U.S. & Soviet Union

India — Viceroy & Governor Generals Archibald Percival Wavell Louis Mountbatten

Ireland — President Seán T. O'Kelly

Italy — Prime Minister Alcide De Gasperi

Japan — Under Allied Occupation
Prime Ministers
Shigeru Yoshida
Tetsu Katayama

Mexico — President
Miguel Alemán Valdés

New Zealand — Prime Minister
Peter Fraser

Pakistan — Governor-General
Muhammad Ali Jinnah

Spain — President
Francisco Franco

South Africa — Prime Minister
Jan Smuts

Soviet Union — Communist Party Leader
Joseph Stalin

EVENTS FROM 1947

JANUARY

15   Elizabeth Short, an aspiring actress nicknamed the "Black Dahlia", is found brutally murdered in a vacant lot in Los Angeles. The case remains unsolved to this day.

25   Gangster Alphonse Gabriel "Al" Capone (born January 17, 1899) suffers a fatal cardiac arrest at his mansion in Palm Island, Florida.

FEBRUARY

3   Percival Prattis becomes the first African-American news correspondent allowed in the United States House of Representatives and Senate press galleries.

17   The Voice Of America begins to transmit radio broadcasts into Eastern Europe and the Soviet Union.

20   An explosion at the O'Connor Electro-Plating Company in Los Angeles, California leaves 17 dead, 100 buildings damaged and a 22 foot deep (6.7m) crater in the ground.

20   Fruit flies become the first living things to be sent into space (and returned). They are accompanied by rye and cotton seeds, and were launched aboard a V-2 rocket by the U.S. Army Ordnance Corps to an altitude of 68 miles (109km).

21   Edwin Land demonstrates the Polaroid Land Camera (the first instant camera) to a meeting of the Optical Society of America in New York.

28   The United States grants France a military base in Casablanca.

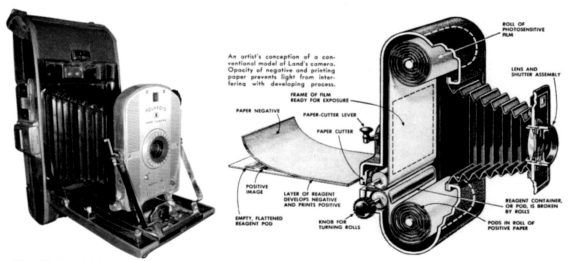

The Polaroid Land Camera Model 95 - The first commercially available instant camera.

By 1948 the 4lb. Polaroid Land Camera Model 95 was on sale at the Jordan Marsh department store in Boston for $89.75. It made more than $5 million in sales in the first year and would be the prototype for Polaroid cameras for the next 15 years.

MARCH

19   The 19th Academy Awards ceremony is held to celebrate the best films of 1946. The movie Best Years of Our Lives wins the Academy Award for Best Picture along with eight other Oscars.

25   A coal mine explosion in Centralia, Illinois, kills 111 miners.

APRIL

1   Jackie Robinson becomes the first African American baseball professional since the 1880s after signing a contract with the Brooklyn Dodgers.

7   American industrialist and the founder of the Ford Motor Company Henry Ford dies (born July 30, 1863). A public viewing was held at Greenfield Village where up to 5,000 people per hour filed past the casket. He was buried in the Ford Cemetery in Detroit.

9   Multiple tornadoes strike Texas, Oklahoma and Kansas killing 181 and injuring 970.

15   Jackie Robinson makes his Major League Baseball debut.

16   Texas City Disaster: The ammonium nitrate cargo of French-registered Liberty ship SS Grandcamp explodes in Texas City, Texas, killing at least 581. All but one member of the city fire department dies, 5,000+ are injured and 20 city blocks are destroyed. Of the dead, remains of 113 are never found and 63 are unidentifiable.

16   American financier and presidential adviser Bernard Baruch first describes the post-World War II tensions between the Soviet Union and the United States as a "Cold War".

26   Academy-Award winning Tom and Jerry cartoon, The Cat Concerto, is released to theatres.

Jackie Robinson signs his Major League Baseball contract with the Brooklyn Dodgers.

On April 15, 1947, 28-year-old Jackie Robinson made his Major League Baseball debut with the Dodgers, against the Boston Braves, in front of more than 25,000 spectators at Ebbets Field in Brooklyn, New York. In his first year Robinson played in 151 games, hit .297, stole more bases than anyone else in the National League and was awarded the first-ever Rookie of the Year title. Robinson became the first African-American inducted into the Baseball Hall of Fame in 1962 in his first year of eligibility. On April 15, 1997 Robinson's jersey number, 42, was retired throughout Major League Baseball.

22 In an effort to fight the spread of Communism President Harry S. Truman signs an Act of Congress that implements the Truman Doctrine. This Act grants $400 million in military and economic aid to Turkey and Greece.

On May 22, 1947 David Lean's film Great Expectations, based on the novel by Charles Dickens, opens in the United States. Starring John Mills as Pip and Valerie Hobson as Estella, critics call it the finest film ever made from a Charles Dickens novel. The film wins 2 Academy Awards and is nominated for 3 others.

JUNE

5 Secretary of State George Marshall outlines the Marshall Plan for American reconstruction and relief aid to Europe.

20 Gangster Bugsy Siegel (born February 28, 1906) is shot dead at the Beverly Hills home of his girlfriend, Virginia Hill.

JUNE

21	Fred Crisman and Harold Dahl claims to have seen six UFOs near Maury Island in Puget Sound, Washington. The next morning Dahl reports the first modern so-called "Men in Black" encounter. Years later Dahl confesses to a reporter that the incident was a hoax.
23	The United States Senate follows the House of Representatives in overriding President Truman's veto of the Taft-Hartley Act that restricted the activities and power of labor unions.
24	Kenneth Arnold makes the first widely reported UFO sighting near Mount Rainier, Washington after claiming to have seen nine unusual objects flying in tandem. The U.S. Air Force formally listed the Arnold case as a mirage.

JULY

Leased Wire
Associated Press

Roswell Daily Record

RECORD PHONES
Business Office 2288
News Department 2287

OL. 47 NUMBER 99 ESTABLISHED 1888   ROSWELL, NEW MEXICO. TUESDAY, JULY 8, 1947   5c PER COPY.

RAAF Captures Flying Saucer On Ranch in Roswell Region

No Details of Flying Disk Are Revealed

Roswell Hardware Man and Wife Report Disk Seen

On July 7, 1947 a supposedly downed extra-terrestrial spacecraft is reported to have been found near Roswell, New Mexico. On July 8 the Roswell Army Air Field public information officer Walter Haut issued a press release stating that personnel from the field's 509th Operations Group had recovered a "flying disc" which had crashed on a ranch near Roswell. Later that day the Commanding General of the Eighth Air Force, Roger Ramey, stated that it was a weather balloon that had been recovered. A press conference was held featuring debris which matched the weather balloon description.

18	President Truman signs the Presidential Succession Act into law which places the Speaker of the House and the President Pro Tempore of the Senate next in the line of succession after the United States Vice President.
26	President Truman signs the National Security Act of 1947 into law thus creating the Central Intelligence Agency, the Department of Defense, the Joint Chiefs of Staff and the National Security Council.

AUGUST

	The Fernwood Park race riot took place between 98th and 111th street in the Fernwood neighbourhood of Roseland, Chicago. It was one of the worst race riots in Chicago's history.
29	The U.S. announced the discovery of plutonium fission (suitable for nuclear power generation).

SEPTEMBER

17 - 21	The 1947 Fort Lauderdale Hurricane hits south-eastern Florida, Alabama, Mississippi and Louisiana causing widespread damage and killing 51 people.

SEPTEMBER

17	The Office of Indian Affairs renamed Bureau of Indian Affairs.
20	Former New York Mayor Fiorello Henry La Guardia dies. Guardia was the 99th Mayor of New York City (for three terms from 1934-45) and became acclaimed as one of the greatest mayors in American history.
26	The U.S. Air Force is made a separate branch of the military.

OCTOBER

Oct - Nov	Forest fires in Maine consume more than 200,000 acres of wooded land state-wide, including over 17,000 acres on Mount Desert Island alone. 16 people are killed and more than 1,000 homes destroyed in the blazes with total property damage exceeding $23 million. The House Un-American Activities Committee begins its investigations into communism in Hollywood.
6	The World Series games are broadcast on television for the first time.

On October 14, 1947 the United States Air Force test pilot Captain Chuck Yeager flew a Bell X-1 rocket plane faster than the speed of sound - the first time that this had been accomplished in level flight. The airplane (nicknamed Glamorous Glennis after his wife) was drop launched from the bomb bay of a modified B-29 Superfortress bomber and reached a speed of Mach 1.06 (700 mph).

20	Pakistan establishes diplomatic relations with the United States.

NOVEMBER

2	In California, designer and airplane pilot Howard Hughes performs the maiden flight of the Spruce Goose which is the largest fixed-wing aircraft ever built. The flight lasts only eight minutes and the Spruce Goose is never flown again.
6	The program Meet The Press makes its television debut on the NBC-TV network. It is currently the longest-running program in U.S. television history.

NOVEMBER

24   The U.S. House of Representatives votes 346-17 to approve citations of Contempt of Congress against the so-called Hollywood 10 after the ten men refuse to co-operate with the House Un-American Activities Committee concerning allegations of communist influences in the movie business. The ten men are blacklisted by the Hollywood movie studios on the following day.

DECEMBER

3   The Tennessee Williams play, A Streetcar Named Desire, opens on Broadway. Later in 1948 the play receives the Pulitzer Prize for Drama and is generally considered to be Williams' greatest piece of work.

22   The first practical electronic transistor is demonstrated by John Bardeen and Walter Brattain working under William Shockley at AT&T's Bell Labs.

10 WORLDWIDE NOTEABLE EVENTS FROM 1947

1. The Zika virus is first isolated from a rhesus macaque in the Zika Forest of Uganda.
2. The first use of defibrillation on a human subject is performed by Claude Beck, a professor of surgery at Case Western Reserve University, Cleveland, Ohio.
3. A prototype AK-47 selective-fire, gas-operated assault rifle is produced in the Soviet Union by Mikhail Kalashnikov.
4. The Sikhote-Alin meteorite, the largest known iron meteorite, falls to earth in Siberia.
5. The Doomsday Clock, a symbolic clock face that represents a countdown to possible global catastrophe, is introduced by The Bulletin of the Atomic Scientists' Science and Security Board. The closer they set the Clock to midnight the closer the scientists believe the world is to global disaster.
6. "Mrs. Ples", the most complete skull of an Australopithecus Africanus specimen ever found in South Africa, is discovered at Sterkfontein by Robert Broom and John T. Robinson.
7. Thor Heyerdahl's balsa-wood raft the Kon-Tiki smashes into the reef at Raroia in the Tuamotu Islands after a 101 day, 4300 mile journey across the Pacific Ocean, thus demonstrating that prehistoric peoples could have travelled from there from South America.
8. The 'GLEEP' (Graphite Low Energy Experimental Pile) experimental nuclear reactor runs for the first time at the Atomic Energy Research Establishment, Harwell, near Oxford, England, and becomes the first nuclear reactor to operate in Western Europe. It had an exceptionally long life for a reactor only being shut down in 1990 after 43 years in service.
9. A moth that became lodged in a relay is found to be the cause of a malfunction in the Harvard Mark II electromechanical computer. It is logged as the "first actual case of a bug being found".
10. The clavioline, an electronic keyboard instrument and a forerunner to the analog synthesizer, is invented by Constant Martin.

U.S. Personalities
Born in 1947

Ann Compton
January 19, 1947

Former news reporter and White House correspondent for ABC News Radio. Whilst reporting for ABC News, Compton has traveled around the globe and through all 50 states with presidents, vice presidents and first ladies through seven presidential campaigns. In June 2000 she was inducted into the Journalism Hall of Fame by the Society of Professional Journalists and on November 5, 2005 she was inducted into the National Radio Hall of Fame.

Michio Kaku
January 24, 1947

Theoretical physicist, futurist, and popularizer of science. Kaku is a professor of theoretical physics at the City College of New York and CUNY Graduate Center. He has made frequent appearances on radio, television and film including hosting several TV specials for the BBC, the Discovery Channel, the History Channel and the Science Channel. He has also written three New York Times best sellers: Physics of the Impossible (2008), Physics of the Future (2011), and The Future of the Mind (2014).

Linda Brown Buck
January 29, 1947

Biologist who was awarded the 2004 Nobel Prize in Physiology or Medicine with Richard Axel for their work on olfactory receptors. She was inducted into the National Academy of Sciences in 2003 and the Institute of Medicine in 2006. She is also a Fellow of the American Association for the Advancement of Science and the American Academy of Arts and Sciences. Buck is currently on the faculty of the Fred Hutchinson Cancer Research Center in Seattle.

Mary Farrah Leni Fawcett
February 2, 1947 -
June 25, 2009

Actress and artist. A four-time Emmy Award nominee and six-time Golden Globe Award nominee, Fawcett rose to international fame when she posed for her iconic red swimsuit poster (which became the best-selling pin-up poster in history). She also starred as private investigator Jill Munroe in the first season of the television series Charlie's Angels (1976-77). In 1996 she was ranked No.26 on TV Guide's "50 Greatest TV stars of All-Time".

James Danforth "Dan" Quayle
February 4, 1947

Politician and the 44th Vice President of the United States who served during the term of President George H. W. Bush (1989-93). He was also a U.S. Representative (1977-81) and U.S. Senator (1981-89) for the state of Indiana. As Vice President Quayle made official visits to 47 countries and was appointed chairman of the National Space Council.

Edward James Olmos
February 24, 1947

Actor and director who is probably best known for his roles as William Adama in the re-imagined Battlestar Galactica, Lieutenant Marty Castillo in Miami Vice, teacher Jaime Escalante in Stand and Deliver, Detective Gaff in Blade Runner (1982) and narrator El Pachuco in both the stage and film versions of Zoot Suit. Olmos was nominated for an Academy Award for Best Actor in a Leading Role for his portrayal of Escalante in the film Stand and Deliver (1988).

Willard Mitt Romney
March 12, 1947

Businessman and politician who is better known as just Mitt Romney. He served as the 70th Governor of Massachusetts from 2003 to 2007 and was the Republican Party's nominee for President of the United States in the 2012 election. Romney was the first Mormon to be a major party presidential nominee and in 2012 Time magazine included him in their List of The 100 Most Influential People in the World.

Glenn Close
March 19, 1947

Actress who is widely regarded as one of the finest actresses of her generation. She has won three Emmy Awards, three Tony Awards and received six Academy Award nominations throughout her career (tying the record for being the actress with the most nominations never to have won an Oscar with Deborah Kerr and Thelma Ritter). Close has also campaigned for many issues such as gay marriage, women's rights and mental health.

Raymond Earl Fosse
April 4, 1947

Former professional baseball player and current television sports color commentator. He played in Major League Baseball as a catcher and was drafted in the first round of the 1965 amateur draft by the Cleveland Indians (the Indians first ever draft pick). Fosse won Gold Glove Awards in 1970 and 1971 and was a World Series Champion in both 1973 and 1974. He has been a television and radio broadcaster for the Oakland Athletics since 1986.

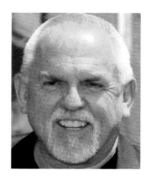

John Dezso Ratzenberger
April 6, 1947

Actor, voice actor and entrepreneur who is best known as Cliff Clavin in Cheers. When auditioning for Cheers he had read for the part of Norm Peterson but had sensed that they weren't going to give him the part. He asked if they had written the part of a bar know-it-all and with that the producers decided it was a great idea and he got the part. Ratzenberger is also known for his extensive vocal work in Pixar movies having had a voice part in every Pixar feature film made to date.

David Michael Letterman
April 12, 1947

Former television talk show host, comedian and producer who hosted a late night television talk show for 33 years. His first show, Late Night with David Letterman on NBC, was broadcast on February 1, 1982 and his final one, Late Show with David Letterman on CBS, ended on May 20, 2015. In total Letterman hosted 6,028 episodes of Late Night and Late Show surpassing friend and mentor Johnny Carson as the longest-serving late night talk show host in American television history.

James Howard Woods
April 18, 1947

Actor and producer who has been nominated for two Academy Awards for his roles in the films Salvador (1986) and Ghosts of Mississippi (1996), and has won three Emmy Awards for the television movies Promise (1986), My Name Is Bill W. (1989) and the animated series Hercules (1998-1999). Woods has also used his distinctive voice to portray animated characters in shows such as The Simpsons and movies such as Stuart Little 2 (2002).

Robert Barton Englund
June 6, 1947

Film and stage actor, voice-actor, singer and director best known for playing the character of infamous serial killer Freddy Krueger in the Nightmare on Elm Street film series. For these he has received a Saturn Award nomination for Best Supporting Actor for A Nightmare on Elm Street 3: Dream Warriors (1987) and A Nightmare on Elm Street 4: The Dream Master (1988). The role catapulted Englund to fame and he became the first new major horror movie star since Sir Christopher Lee and Peter Cushing in the 1960s.

Orenthal James "O. J." Simpson
July 9, 1947

Nicknamed The Juice, Simpson is a former football player, broadcaster and actor. He played professionally in the NFL as a running back for 11 seasons and holds the record for the single season yards-per-game average which stands at 143.1. He was inducted into the College Football Hall of Fame in 1983 and the Pro Football Hall of Fame in 1985. Simpson was convicted of felonies including armed robbery and kidnapping in 2008 and is currently serving 33 years at the Lovelock Correctional Center, in Lovelock Nevada.

Arnold Schwarzenegger
July 30, 1947

Austrian-American actor, producer, businessman, investor, author, philanthropist, activist, former bodybuilder and politician. He began weight training at the age of 15, won the Mr. Universe title at age 20 and went on to win the Mr. Olympia contest 7 times. Schwarzenegger gained worldwide fame as a Hollywood action film icon in movies such as Commando (1985), Predator (1987), True Lies (1994) and the Terminator series of films. From 2003-11 he served two terms as the 38th Governor of California.

Carol Elizabeth Moseley Braun
August 16, 1947

Politician and lawyer who represented Illinois in the U.S. Senate from 1993-99. She was the first (and to date the only) female African-American Senator, the first woman to defeat an incumbent U.S. Senator in an election and the first (and again the only) female Senator from Illinois. From 1999-2001 she was the U.S. Ambassador to New Zealand and during the 2004 U.S. presidential election was a candidate for the Democratic nomination.

Jane Therese Curtin
September 6, 1947

Actress and comedian who is sometimes referred to as "Queen of the Deadpan". She first came to prominence as an original cast member on the hit TV comedy series Saturday Night Live in 1975. She went on to win back-to-back Emmy Awards for Best Lead Actress in a Comedy Series on the 1980s sitcom Kate & Allie. Curtin later starred in the hit series 3rd Rock from the Sun (1996-2001) and has also appeared in many movie roles including the part of Charlene in the The Librarian series of movies (2004–2008).

Lynn Rene Anderson
September 26, 1947 -
July 30, 2015

Country music singer known most notably for her 1970 worldwide hit, I Never Promised You A Rose Garden. Anderson became one of the most popular and successful country singers of the 1970s charting 12 No.1 and more than 50 Top 40 hit singles. In addition to being named Top Female Vocalist by the Academy of Country Music twice she was also named Female Vocalist Of The Year by the Country Music Association. Anderson also won a Grammy Award, a People's Choice Award and an American Music Award.

Kevin Delaney Kline
October 24, 1947

Film and stage actor, comedian and singer. Kline began his career on stage in 1972 with The Acting Company and went on to win two Tony Awards for his work in Broadway musicals. His film debut came opposite Meryl Streep in Sophie's Choice (1982) and for his role in the comedy hit, A Fish Called Wanda (1988), he won the Academy Award for Best Supporting Actor. In 2003 Kline was inducted into the American Theatre Hall of Fame.

Hillary Diane Rodham Clinton
October 26, 1947

Politician and nominee of the Democratic Party for President of the United States in the November 8, 2016 election. She has served as the 67th U.S. Secretary of State (2009-13), the junior U.S. Senator representing New York (2001-09) and First Lady of the United States during the presidency of husband Bill Clinton (1993-2001). On July 28, 2016 Clinton became the first female candidate to be nominated for President by a major U.S. political party.

Richard Stephen Dreyfuss
October 29, 1947

Actor best known for starring in American Graffiti (1973), Jaws (1975), Close Encounters Of The Third Kind (1977), The Goodbye Girl (1977), Stand By Me (1986), Down And Out In Beverly Hills (1986) and Mr. Holland's Opus (1995). Dreyfuss won an Academy Award, Golden Globe and BAFTA for Best Actor in The Goodbye Girl and for his role as Glenn Holland in Mr. Holland's Opus was nominated for both an Academy Award and Golden Globe Award for Best Actor.

William Dwight Schultz
November 24, 1947

Actor and voice artist who is known for his roles as Captain "Howling Mad" Murdock on the 1980s action series The A-Team, and as Reginald Barclay in Star Trek: The Next Generation, Star Trek: Voyager and the film Star Trek: First Contact (1996). He is also well known in animation as the mad scientist Dr. Animo in the Ben 10 series, Chef Mung Daal in the children's cartoon Chowder and as Eddie the Squirrel in CatDog.

John Bernard Larroquette
November 25, 1947

Film and television actor whose roles include Dan Fielding on the 1984-92 sitcom Night Court (winning a then-unprecedented four consecutive Emmy Awards for his role), Mike McBride in the Hallmark Channel series McBride, John Hemingway on The John Larroquette Show, Lionel Tribbey on The West Wing and Carl Sack in Boston Legal. He is currently playing Jenkins/Galahad in TNT's The Librarians.

Edward Bridge "Ted" Danson III
December 29, 1947

Actor, author and producer well known for his role as lead character Sam Malone on the NBC sitcom Cheers and for his role as Dr. John Becker on the CBS sitcom Becker. In his 40-year career, Danson has been nominated for 15 Primetime Emmy Awards, winning two, and ten Golden Globe Awards nominations, winning three. Danson has also been a longtime activist in ocean conservation and in March 2011 published his first book, Oceana: Our Endangered Oceans and What We Can Do to Save Them.

POPULAR MUSIC 1947

No.1	Francis Craig	Near You
No.2	Vaughn Monroe	Ballerina
No.3	Perry Como	Chi-Baba, Chi-Baba
No.4	Tex Williams	Smoke! Smoke! Smoke!
No.5	Jerry Murad's Harmonicats	Peg O' My Heart
No.6	Ted Weems	Heartaches
No.7	Count Basie	Open The Door, Richard!
No.8	Frankie Laine	That's My Desire
No.9	Frank Sinatra	Mam'selle
No.10	Ray Noble	Linda

Francis Craig
Near You

Label:	Written by:	Length:
Bullet Records	Francis Craig / Kermit Goell	2 mins 39 secs

Francis Craig (September 10, 1900 - November 19, 1966) was a songwriter and dance band leader. "Near You" stayed in the music charts for 21 weeks, holding the No.1 spot for 17 weeks and selling over 2.5 million copies. Craig's version of the song was the first pop hit record ever to come out of Nashville, Tennessee and was awarded a gold disc by the RIAA.

Vaughn Monroe
Ballerina

Label:	Written by:	Length:
RCA Victor	Bob Russell / Carl Sigman	3 mins 27 secs

Vaughn Wilton Monroe (October 7, 1911 - May 21, 1973) was a baritone singer, trumpeter, big band leader and actor whose popularity was at its height in the 1940s and 1950s. Monroe formed his first orchestra in Boston in 1940 and became its principal vocalist. He has two stars on the Hollywood Walk of Fame, one for recording and one for radio.

Perry Como
Chi-Baba, Chi-Baba

Label:	Written by:	Length:
RCA Victor	Hoffman / Livingston / David	2 mins 56 secs

Pierino Ronald "Perry" Como (May 18, 1912 - May 12, 2001) was a singer and television personality. During a career spanning more than half a century he recorded exclusively for RCA Victor after signing with the label in 1943. "Mr. C.", as he was nicknamed, sold millions of records for RCA and pioneered a weekly musical variety television show which set the standards for the genre and proved to be one of the most successful in television history.

Tex Williams & The Western Caravan
Smoke! Smoke! Smoke! (That Cigarette)

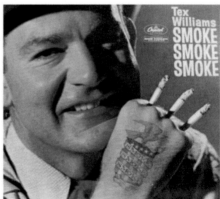

Label:	Written by:	Length:
Capitol	Merle Travis / Tex Williams	2 mins 56 secs

Sollie Paul "Tex" Williams (August 23, 1917 - October 11, 1985) was a Western swing musician who is best known for his talking blues style. His biggest hit was "Smoke! Smoke! Smoke! (That Cigarette)" which held the No.1 position on the Billboard charts for sixteen weeks in 1947 and was No.1 on the country chart that year.

5 Jerry Murad's Harmonicats
Peg O' My Heart

Label:	Written by:	Length:
Vitacoustic	Alfred Bryan / Fred Fisher	2 mins 14 secs

Jerry Murad's Harmonicats were a harmonica-based group. The band was founded in 1947 and consisted of Jerry Murad (chromatic lead harmonica), Don Les (bass harmonica) and Al Fiore (chord harmonica). It was "Peg O' My Heart" that first brought them to public attention and it went on to sell over one million copies.

6 Ted Weems
Heartaches

Label:	Written by:	Length:
RCA Victor / Decca	Al Hoffman / John Klenner	2 mins 40 secs

Wilfred Theodore "Ted" Weems (September 26, 1901 - May 6, 1963) was a bandleader and musician. Heartaches was recorded by his Orchestra in 1933 but it wasn't until 1947 when disc jockey Kurt Webster started playing it again that it reached Billboard magazine's Best Seller chart. The record stayed in the charts for 16 weeks and peaked at No.1.

⑦ Count Basie
Open The Door, Richard!

Label:	Written by:	Length:
RCA Victor	Frank Clarke / Jack McVea	2 mins 44 secs

William James "Count" Basie (August 21, 1904 - April 26, 1984) was a jazz pianist, organist, bandleader and composer. Basie formed his jazz orchestra, the Count Basie Orchestra, in 1935 and led the group for almost 50 years. "Open The Door, Richard" was recorded by a number of other artists in 1947 but the Count Basie version was the most successful.

⑧ Frankie Laine
That's My Desire

Label:	Written by:	Length:
Mercury	Carroll Loveday / Helmy Kresa	2 mins 52 secs

Frankie Laine (born Francesco Paolo LoVecchio; March 30, 1913 - February 6, 2007) was a singer, songwriter and actor whose career spanned 75 years from his first concerts in 1930 to his final performance of "That's My Desire" in 2005. "That's My Desire" was Laine's first chart hit and peaked at No.4 in June 1947.

Frank Sinatra
Mam'selle

Label:	Written by:	Length:
Columbia	Edmund Goulding / Mack Gordon	3 mins 18 secs

Francis Albert "Frank" Sinatra (December 12, 1915 - May 14, 1998) was a singer, actor, director and producer who is one of the best-selling music artists of all time having sold more than 150 million records worldwide. Sinatra was awarded the U.S. Presidential Medal of Freedom by Ronald Reagan in 1985 and the Congressional Gold Medal in 1997.

Ray Noble
Linda

Label:	Written by:	Length:
Columbia	Jack Lawrence	3 mins 11 secs

Raymond Stanley "Ray" Noble (December 17, 1903 - April 3, 1978) was a bandleader, composer, arranger, radio comedian and actor. "Linda" was written in 1942 after the one-year-old daughter of Jack Lawrence's attorney, Linda Eastman (who later married Beatle Paul McCartney). In 1987 Noble was inducted into the Big Band and Jazz Hall of Fame, and in 1996 he was inducted into the Songwriters Hall of Fame.

TOP FILMS 1947

1. Unconquered
2. The Bachelor And The Bobby-Soxer
3. The Egg And I
4. Mother Wore Tights
5. Life With Father

OSCARS

Best Film: Gentleman's Agreement

Best Director: Elia Kazan
(Gentleman's Agreement)
Best Actor: Ronald Colman
(A Double Life)
Best Actress: Loretta Young
(The Farmer's Daughter)
Best Supporting Actor: Edmund Gwenn
(Miracle on 34th Street)
Best Supporting Actress: Celeste Holm
(Gentleman's Agreement)

UNCONQUERED

Directed by: Cecil B. DeMille - Runtime: 146 minutes

Intrepid frontiersman Chris Holden foils the political and personal ambitions of renegade Martin Garth in the Ohio Valley following the French and Indian War.

Gross: $6,100,000

STARRING

Gary Cooper
Born: May 7, 1901
Died: May 13, 1961

Character:
Capt. Christopher Holden

Film actor born Frank James Cooper. His career spanned 35 years (1925-1960) and included leading roles in 84 feature films. Cooper received the Academy Award for Best Actor for his roles in Sergeant York (1941) and High Noon (1952). He also received an Honorary Award for his career achievements in 1961. The American Film Institute also ranked Cooper 11th greatest male star of classic Hollywood cinema.

Paulette Goddard
Born: June 3, 1910
Died: April 23, 1990

Character:
Abby

Goddard was a child fashion model and performer who became a major star for Paramount Studios in the 1940s. Her most notable films were as Charles Chaplin's leading lady in Modern Times (her first major role) and his subsequent film The Great Dictator (1940). She was nominated for an Academy Award for Best Supporting Actress for her performance in So Proudly We Hail! (1943).

Howard Da Silva
Born: May 4, 1909
Died: February 16, 1986

Character:
Garth

Actor, director and musical performer on stage, film, television and radio. He was cast in dozens of productions on the New York stage, appeared in more than two dozen television programs and acted in more than 50 feature films. Adept at both drama and musicals on the stage he appeared in the original 1943 run of the Rodgers and Hammerstein musical Oklahoma!

TRIVIA

Goofs

During the rapids chase six Senecas occupy each of two long canoes. Later in the chase the canoes are shorter and hold only three men apiece.

When going over the waterfall support wires can be seen on the actors.

Interesting Facts

While Boris Karloff was filming his scenes he had his customary 4:00pm tea break which he always had written into his contract. They became so popular that even Gary Cooper and Charles Chaplin came on set for tea, and Paulette Goddard had a 4:00pm tea break written into her contracts for the rest of her career.

The film went $394,000 over budget.

The film features 25 named actors and 4,325 costumed extras.

Interesting Facts   The famous Swedish actor Edvard Persson was travelling through the US to make Jens Månsson i Amerika (1947) when he came to Hollywood and made a cameo appearance in this film. Director Cecil B. DeMille reciprocated with a cameo appearance in Persson's movie.

Gary Cooper got a salary of $300,000 for this film which was double what he usually made.

Cecil B. DeMille became enraged at Paulette Goddard when she refused to do a stunt that required her to have fireballs thrown at her. DeMille was forced to use a stuntwoman, who got burned. Five years later he was making The Greatest Show on Earth (1952) when he reportedly had his revenge by turning down Goddard's acceptance of a key role by replacing her with Gloria Grahame.

This film marked the 20th anniversary of Gary Cooper's contract with Paramount and it was also his last film for the studio.

THE BACHELOR AND THE BOBBY-SOXER

Directed by: Irving Reis - Runtime: 95 minutes

Teenaged Susan Turner has a crush on playboy artist Richard Nugent and sneaks into his apartment to model for him. She is found there by her sister Judge Margaret Turner and Nugent is threatened with jail. He agrees to date Susan until the crush abates and counters her comic false sophistication by even more comic put-on teenage mannerisms.

Gross: $5,500,000

STARRING

Cary Grant
Born: January 18, 1904
Died: November 29, 1986

Character:
Richard Nugent

British-American actor known as one of classic Hollywood's definitive leading men. He began a career in Hollywood in the early 1930s and became known for his transatlantic accent, light-hearted approach to acting, comic timing and debonair demeanour. He was twice nominated for the Academy Award for Best Actor for his roles in Penny Serenade (1941) and None But The Lonely Heart (1944).

Myrna Loy
Born: August 2, 1905
Died: December 14, 1993

Character:
Judge Margaret Turner

Film, television and stage actress who trained as a dancer. Although originally typecast in earlier films her career took off following her portrayal of Nora Charles in The Thin Man (1934). In March 1991 Loy was presented with an Honorary Academy Award with the inscription 'In recognition of her extraordinary qualities both on screen and off, with appreciation for a lifetime's worth of indelible performances.'

Shirley Temple
Born: April 23, 1928
Died: February 10, 2014

Character:
Susan Turner

American film and television actress, singer, dancer and public servant. Temple began her film career in 1932 at the age of three and was Hollywood's number one box-office star from 1935 through 1938. As an adult she entered politics and became a diplomat serving as US Ambassador to Ghana and later to Czechoslovakia. She also served as Chief of Protocol of the United States.

TRIVIA

Goofs

When the main characters arrive at the picnic in a jalopy the windshield is folded down but when they get out it's back up.

A reflection of boom mic is visible in the black car when it pulls up to the airport.

Interesting Facts

Myrna Loy was almost 23 years older than her on-screen sister Shirley Temple.

"The Screen Guild Theater" broadcast a 30 minute radio adaptation of the movie on May 10, 1948 with Cary Grant, Myrna Loy and Shirley Temple reprising their film roles.

CONTINUED

Interesting Facts   The "man with the power" rhyming routine was adapted into the song lyric of The Atomic Fireballs' song "Man With the Hex" during the Swing Revival of the 1990s. It was also the inspiration for the song "Magic Dance" in the movie Labyrinth (1986).

Quotes

Richard: Hey, you remind me of a man.
Susan: What man?
Richard: Man with the power.
Susan: What power?
Richard: Power of hoodoo.
Susan: Hoodoo?
Richard: You do.
Susan: Do what?
Richard: Remind me of a man...

Susan: Did you have many ordeals before you became a success?
Richard: No, I...
Susan: You can talk to me. I want you to think of me, not as a newspaper woman, but as a friend.
Richard: Well, in that case, I'll tell you. I did suffer. When I was 10, my mother and father had a double suicide pact, they made it. I was sent to an orphanage. Some days they didn't beat me. Then one night I escaped, I ran away to New York. I used to steal.
Susan: What did you steal?
Richard: Beg your pardon?
Susan: What did you steal?
Richard: Crusts of bread... and things. One time I stole a valise. There were paints and paintbrushes inside. So I began to paint. Then they got me. I was sent to a reform school but I escaped again.
Susan: Go on.
Richard: Back to New York. A wealthy society lady saw my work, fell in love with me and sent me to art school. The rest is history.
Susan: How wonderful. How terribly wonderful.

Susan: You're going to make me an old maid.
Margaret: Only until you're 18.

THE EGG AND I

Directed by: Chester Erskine - Runtime: 108 minutes

On their wedding night Bob informs his new bride Betty that he has bought a chicken farm (an abandoned chicken farm to be exact which becomes obvious when the two move in). Betty endures Bob's enthusiasm for the rural life but her patience is severely tested when glamorous neighbor Harriet Putnam seems to set her sights on Bob.

Gross: $5,500,000

STARRING

Claudette Colbert
Born: September 13, 1903
Died: July 30, 1996

Character:
Betty MacDonald

Actress and a leading lady in Hollywood for over two decades. Colbert began her career in Broadway productions during the late 1920s and progressed to film with the advent of talking pictures. She won the Academy Award for Best Actress in It Happened One Night (1934) and starred in more than sixty movies during her career. She was the industry's biggest box-office star in both 1938 and 1942.

Fred MacMurray
Born: August 30, 1908
Died: November 5, 1991

Character:
Bob MacDonald

Actor who appeared in more than 100 films during a career that spanned nearly half a century (from 1930 to the 1970s). MacMurray is best known for his roles in the film Double Indemnity (1944) directed by Billy Wilder, for his performances in numerous Disney films including The Absent-Minded Professor and The Shaggy Dog, and as Steve Douglas in the television series My Three Sons, which ran from 1960 to 1972.

Marjorie Main
Born: February 24, 1890
Died: April 10, 1975

Character:
Phoebe 'Ma' Kettle

Character actress who initially worked in vaudeville, debuting on Broadway in 1916, before her first film A House Divided (1931). Perhaps her most famous role is that of Ma Kettle which she first played in The Egg and I opposite Percy Kilbride as Pa Kettle. She was nominated for an Academy Award for Best Actress in a Supporting Role for the part and portrayed the character in nine more Ma and Pa Kettle films.

TRIVIA

Interesting Facts

This is the first of seven films pairing Claudette Colbert and Fred MacMurray.

This comedy was such a hit with audiences it spawned the Ma and Pa Kettle film series.

"The Hedda Hopper Show - This Is Hollywood" broadcast a 30 minute radio adaptation of the movie on January 4, 1947 with Claudette Colbert. The adaptation was unusual in that it preceded the film's release.

The road in the U.S. state of Washington, where the farm once owned by the Egg And I book author Betty MacDonald (1907-1958) was located, was named The Egg And I Road on February 3, 1981.

CONTINUED

Interesting Facts   The Egg and I was first published in 1945 and contains the humorous memoirs of author Betty MacDonald about her adventures and travels as a young wife on a chicken farm on the Olympic Peninsula in Washington state. The book is based on the author's experiences as a newlywed in trying to acclimate and operate a small chicken farm with her first husband Robert Heskett from 1927 to 1931. On visits with her family in Seattle she told stories of their tribulations which greatly amused them. In the 1940s MacDonald's sisters strongly encouraged her to write a book about these experiences. The Egg and I was MacDonald's first attempt at writing a book.

Quotes   **Betty MacDonald:** I bet you think an egg is something you casually order for breakfast when you can't think of anything else. Well, so did I once, but that was before the egg and I.

MOTHER WORE TIGHTS

Directed by: Walter Lang - Runtime: 107 minutes

The chronicles of a vaudeville family during the early 1900s as they struggle to bring up a family and tour the nation.

Gross: $5,250,000

STARRING

Elizabeth Ruth "Betty" Grable
Born: December 18, 1916
Died: July 2, 1973

Character:
Myrtle McKinley/Burt

Actress, pin-up model, dancer and singer who began her film career in 1929 at age 12 and whose 42 movies during the 1930s and 1940s grossed more than $100 million. She set a record of 12 consecutive years in the top 10 of box office stars and the U.S. Treasury Department listed her as the highest-salaried American woman in 1946-47. Grable has a star on the Hollywood Walk of Fame and also on the St. Louis Walk of Fame.

Daniel James "Dan" Dailey
Born: December 14, 1915
Died: October 16, 1978

Character:
Frank Burt

Dancer and actor who appeared in vaudeville before his Broadway debut in 1937 in Babes in Arms. In 1940 he was signed by MGM to make films. He served in the U.S. Army during World War II and was commissioned as an Army officer. Dailey returned to Hollywood after the war and his performance with Betty Grable in When My Baby Smiles At Me (1948) earned him an Academy Award nomination for Best Actor.

Monica Elizabeth "Mona" Freeman
Born: June 9, 1926
Died: May 23, 2014

Character:
Iris Burt

Portrait painter, television and film actress. Freeman was a model whilst in high school and after becoming the first "Miss Subways" for the New York City transit system, signed a movie contract with Howard Hughes. Her first film appearance was in the 1944 film Till We Meet Again. She soon became a popular teenage movie star but as an adult Freeman's career slowed and she appeared in mostly B-movies and in several guest roles on television.

TRIVIA

Interesting Facts

This was the first of four movies that paired Betty Grable and Dan Dailey - the other films were When My Baby Smiles At Me (1948), My Blue Heaven (1950) and Call Me Mister (1951).

Betty Grable was pregnant with her second child Jessica James during the filming of this movie.

Of all her films this was reportedly Betty Grable's favorite.

Lux Radio Theater broadcast a 60 minute radio adaptation of this movie on February 2, 1948 with Betty Grable and Dan Daily reprising their film roles.

Non singing star Mona Freeman was dubbed by Imogene Lynn.

CONTINUED

Interesting Facts   Twentieth Century-Fox had wanted either James Cagney or Fred Astaire to play the role of song-and-dance man Frank Burt. After negotiations with Fred Astaire fell through Betty Grable requested John Payne who already had appeared with her in a number of films. The role eventually went to Dan Dailey.

The complete performance by Betty Grable and Dan Dailey of "On A Little Two-Seat Tandem" was cut from the film and all that remains is a partial song-and-dance reprise near the end of the movie.

Mother Wore Tights won the Academy Award for Best Score and was nominated for the Academy Awards for Best Cinematography and Best Song.

The film was based on the book "Mother Wore Tights" by Miriam Young and was her memoir of growing up in a vaudeville family.

Director Walter Lang started his career in 1925 with the silent film The Red Kimono but when hired by 20th Century Fox in the mid-1930s he directed a number of the spectacular colorful musicals for which Fox Studios became famous for producing during the 1940s. One of Lang's most recognized films is his 1956 epic The King and I for which he was nominated for the Academy Award for Directing.

LIFE WITH FATHER

Directed by: Michael Curtiz - Runtime: 118 minutes

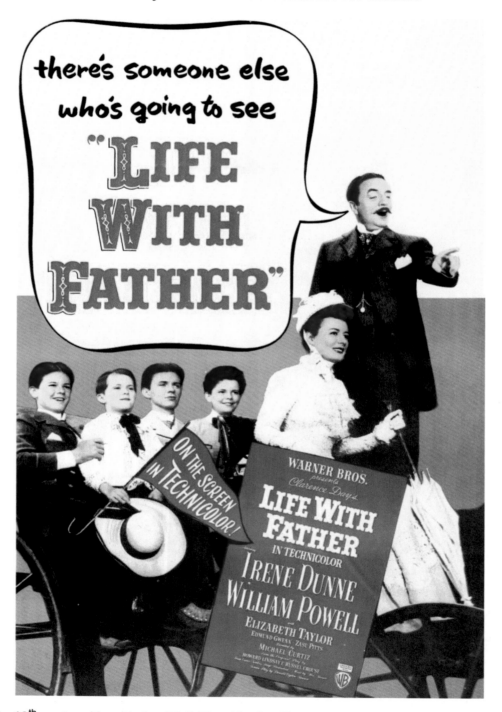

In late 19th century New York a Wall Street broker likes to think his house runs his way but finds himself constantly bemused at how much of what happens is down to his wife.

Gross: $5,057,000

STARRING

William Powell
Born: July 29, 1892
Died: March 5, 1984

Character:
Clarence Day (Father)

Actor William Horatio Powell was a major star at Metro-Goldwyn-Mayer. He was paired with Myrna Loy in 14 of his films including the popular Thin Man series based on the Nick and Nora Charles characters created by Dashiell Hammett. Powell was nominated for the Academy Award for Best Actor three times including, The Thin Man (1934), My Man Godfrey (1936) and Life With Father.

Irene Dunne
Born: December 20, 1898
Died: September 4, 1990

Character:
Vinnie

Actress and singer of the 1930s, 1940s and early 1950s. Dunne was nominated five times for the Academy Award for Best Actress for her performances in Cimarron (1931), Theodora Goes Wild (1936), The Awful Truth (1937), Love Affair (1939) and I Remember Mama (1948). In 1985 Dunne was given Kennedy Center Honors for her lifetime of contributions to American culture.

Elizabeth Taylor
Born: February 27, 1932
Died: March 23, 2011

Character:
Mary

Dame Elizabeth Taylor was a British-American actress who from her early years as a child star with MGM became one of the greatest screen actresses of Hollywood's Golden Age. She won her first Oscar for Best Actress for BUtterfield 8 in 1960. Later, after playing the title role in Cleopatra (1963), she married her co-star Richard Burton and they appeared together in 11 films including Who's Afraid of Virginia Woolf? for which Taylor won a second Academy Award.

TRIVIA

Goofs

The opening scene shows a carriage block with "Clarence Day" engraved on it. A few seconds later, after the police man passes by, the carriage block has no engraving.

Clarence Jr. says to his brother Whitney (as he is reading the paper) that Buck Ewing of the New York Giants hit a home run. In 1883 (the year the film is set) the team was called the New York Gothams and it was only in 1885 that the team's name was changed to Giants.

When Vinnie is ill Dr. Humphries goes out and brings back Dr. Somers. When they go upstairs Dr. Somers leads but in the next shot he is behind Dr. Humphries.

Interesting Facts

Other than the color scenes in Leathernecking (1930) this was Irene Dunne's only film in color.

CONTINUED

Interesting Facts   Mary Pickford made several tests for the role of Vinnie but the studio worried about her popularity after a 13-year absence from the screen. In the end director Michael Curtiz vetoed her for the box-office appeal of Irene Dunne.

Before filming began the cast was taken to Perc Westmore's salon on a Sunday morning to have their hair dyed red. When it was time to rinse the dye the beauticians discovered that the water had been turned off for the entire block because the street was being repaired. Due to the dyes being so strong back then leaving them on could have caused the cast to all lose their hair. Luckily someone suggested diluting the dye with cold cream.

The movie premiere was held on August 14, 1947 in Skowhegan, Maine, where the play had its first performance eight years earlier. The stage play (based on Clarence Day's book) ran 3,224 performances, holding the record for the longest non-musical run on Broadway.

Quotes   **Vinnie:** That's the loveliest ring you ever bought me. Now that I have this, you needn't buy me any more rings.
Father: Well, if you don't want anymore ...
Vinnie: What I'd really like now is a nice diamond necklace.

Father: They can't keep me out of heaven on a technicality!

Sporting Winners

Johnny Lujack - College Football

Associated Press - Male Athlete Of The Year

JOHNNY LUJACK *Quarterback*

John Christopher Lujack Jr.
Born: January 4, 1925 in Connellsville, Pennsylvania
Position: Quarterback / Defensive Back - NFL Draft: 1946 / Round: 1 / Pick: 4

Johnny Lujack was a former American football quarterback and 1947 Heisman Trophy winner. He played college football for the University of Notre Dame and professionally for the Chicago Bears. Lujack was the first of several successful quarterbacks who hailed from Western Pennsylvania (others include Pro Football Hall of Fame members Johnny Unitas, Joe Namath, Dan Marino, Jim Kelly, Joe Montana and George Blanda).

Career Highlights:

3× National Champion (1943, 1946, 1947)
2× Unanimous All-American (1946, 1947)
Heisman Trophy (1947)
Sporting News Player Of The Year (1947)
Associated Press Athlete Of The Year (1947)
3× First-Team All-Pro (1948-1950)
NFL Passing Yards Leader (1949)
NFL Passing Touchdowns Leader (1949)
NFL Rushing Touchdowns Leader (1950)
2× Pro Bowl (1950, 1951)
Second-Team All-Pro (1951)

Lujacks career was interrupted for two years during World War II (1944-1945) while he served as an officer in the United States Navy hunting German submarines in the English Channel.

BABE DIDRIKSON ZAHARIAS - GOLF

ASSOCIATED PRESS - FEMALE ATHLETE OF THE YEAR

Mildred Ella Didrikson Zaharias
Born: June 26, 1911 in Port Arthur, Texas
Died: September 27, 1956 in Galveston, Texas
Professional golfer from 1947 until her death in 1956

Zaharias was athlete who achieved a great deal of success in golf, basketball, baseball and track and field. At the 1932 Los Angeles Olympics she equalled the world record of 11.8 seconds in her opening heat in the 80 meter hurdles and in the final she broke her record with 11.7 seconds to take the gold. In the javelin she also won gold with an Olympic record throw of 43.69 meters and took silver with a world record-tying leap of 1.657 metres (5.44 ft) in the High Jump.

It wasn't until 1935 that she began to play golf, eventually becoming America's first female golf celebrity and the leading player of the 1940s and early 1950s. In 1946 she won the U.S. Women's Amateur Golf Championship and the 1947 British Ladies Amateur Golf Championship becoming the first American to do so. Zaharias won 17 straight women's amateur victories - a feat that has never been equalled. Having formally turned professional in 1947 she dominated the golfing tournaments ran by the Women's Professional Golf Association and later the Ladies Professional Golf Association (of which she was a founding member). In 1948 she became the first woman to attempt to qualify for the U.S. Open but her application was rejected by the USGA - they stated that the event was intended to be open to men only. By 1950 she had won every golf title available. Totalling both her amateur and professional victories Zaharias won an incredible 82 golf tournaments.

Major championships:

Women's Western Open	1940	1944	1945	1950
Titleholders Championship	1947	1950	1952	
U.S. Womens Open	1948	1950	1954	

Zaharias was the winner of the Associated Press Female Athlete of the Year a total of six times; 1932, 1945, 1946, 1947, 1950 and 1954.

GOLF

THE MASTERS - JIMMY DEMARET

The Masters Tournament is the first of the majors to be played each year and unlike the other major championships it is played at the same location - Augusta National Golf Club, Georgia. This was the 11th Masters Tournament and was held April 3-6 with 1940 Champion Jimmy Demaret winning the second of his three Masters titles. The total prize fund was $10,000 with Demaret taking home $2,500.

U.S. OPEN - LEW WORSHAM

The U.S. Open Championship (established in 1895) was held June 12-15 at St. Louis Country Club in Ladue, Missouri, a suburb west of St. Louis. Lew Worsham won his only major title denying Sam Snead his elusive U.S. Open title by prevailing in an 18-hole playoff. His share of the $10,000 purse was $2,500 with runner up Sam Snead receiving $2,000.

PGA CHAMPIONSHIP - JIM FERRIER

The 1947 and 29th PGA Championship was played June 18-24 at Plum Hollow Country Club in Southfield, Michigan, a suburb northwest of Detroit. Jim Ferrier won the match play championship 2 & 1 over Chick Harbert to take his only major title. The total prize fund was $17,700 with the winner's share being $3,500.

WORLD SERIES - NEW YORK YANKEES

New York Yankees **4 - 3** **Brooklyn Dodgers**

Total attendance: 389,763 - Average attendance: 55,680
Winning player's share: $5,830 - Losing player's share: $4,081

The World Series is the annual championship series of Major League Baseball, played since 1903 between the American League (AL) champion team and the National League (NL) champion, and is determined through a best-of-seven playoff.

The 1947 World Series matched the New York Yankees against the Brooklyn Dodgers. The Yankees won the Series in seven games for their first title since 1943 and their eleventh World Series Championship. Yankees manager Bucky Harris won for the first time since managing the Washington Senators to their only title win in 1924.

	Date	Score	Location	Time	Att.
1	Sep 30	Brooklyn Dodgers - 3 **New York Yankees - 5**	Yankee Stadium	2:20	73,365
2	Oct 1	Brooklyn Dodgers - 3 **New York Yankees - 10**	Yankee Stadium	2:36	69,865
3	Oct 2	New York Yankees - 8 **Brooklyn Dodgers - 9**	Ebbets Field	3:05	33,098
4	Oct 3	New York Yankees - 2 **Brooklyn Dodgers - 3**	Ebbets Field	2:20	33,443
5	Oct 4	**New York Yankees - 2** Brooklyn Dodgers - 1	Ebbets Field	2:46	34,379
6	Oct 5	**Brooklyn Dodgers - 8** New York Yankees - 6	Yankee Stadium	3:19	74,065
7	Oct 6	Brooklyn Dodgers - 2 **New York Yankees - 5**	Yankee Stadium	2:19	71,548

HORSE RACING

1947 American Champion Three-Year-Old Male Horse Phalanx.

Phalanx (1944-1971) was an American Champion thoroughbred racehorse. In 1947 he won the Belmont Stakes by five lengths, came second the Kentucky Derby and third in the Preakness Stakes. He also won the Dwyer Stakes, the Empire City Handicap and in the fall, the two-mile Jockey Club Gold Cup. During his career Phalanx earned a total of $409,275.

KENTUCKY DERBY - JET PILOT

The Kentucky Derby is held annually at Churchill Downs in Louisville, Kentucky on the first Saturday in May. The race is a Grade I stakes race for three-year-olds and is one and a quarter miles in length.

PREAKNESS STAKES - FAULTLESS

The Preakness Stakes is held on the third Saturday in May each year at Pimlico Race Course in Baltimore, Maryland. It is a Grade I race run over a distance of 9.5 furlongs (1 3/16 miles) on dirt.

BELMONT STAKES - PHALANX

The Belmont Stakes is Grade I race held every June at Belmont Park in Elmont, New York. It is 1.5 miles in length and open to three-year-old thoroughbreds. It takes place on a Saturday between June 5 and June 11.

FOOTBALL - NFL CHAMPIONSHIP

CHAMPIONSHIP GAME

Philadelphia Eagles   21 - 28   **Chicago Cardinals**

Played: December 28, 1947 at Comiskey Park, Chicago, Illinois.
Attendance: 30,759

The 1947 NFL season was the 28th regular season of the National Football League. The league expanded the regular season from eleven to twelve games per team with the number of games then remaining constant for the next fourteen seasons until 1960. The season ended when the Chicago Cardinals defeated the Philadelphia Eagles in the NFL Championship Game.

Conference Results:

Eastern Conference

Team	P	W	L	T	PCT	PF	PA
Philadelphia Eagles	**12**	**8**	**4**	**0**	**.667**	**308**	**242**
Pittsburgh Steelers	12	8	4	0	.667	240	259
Boston Yanks	12	4	7	1	.364	168	256
Washington Redskins	12	4	8	0	.333	295	367
New York Giants	12	2	8	2	.200	190	309

Western Conference

Team	P	W	L	T	PCT	PF	PA
Chicago Cardinals	**12**	**9**	**3**	**0**	**.750**	**306**	**231**
Chicago Bears	12	8	4	0	.667	363	241
Green Bay Packers	12	6	5	1	.545	274	210
Los Angeles Rams	12	6	6	0	.500	259	214
Detroit Lions	12	3	9	0	.250	231	305

P= Games Played, W = Wins, L = Losses, T = Ties,
PCT= Winning Percentage, PF= Points For, PA = Points Against

League Leaders

Statistic	Name	Team	Yards
Passing Yards	Sammy Baugh	Washington Redskins	2938
Rushing Yards	Steve Van Buren	Philadelphia Eagles	1008
Receiving Yards	Mal Kutner	Chicago Cardinals	944
Total Points Scored	Pat Harder	Chicago Cardinals	102

HOCKEY: 1946-47 NHL SEASON

The 1946-47 NHL season was the 30th season of the National Hockey League with six teams each playing 60 games. The season ended when the Toronto Maple Leafs defeated the Montreal Canadiens in the 1947 Stanley Cup Final to win their sixth Stanley Cup.

Final Standings:

		GP	W	L	T	GF	GA	Pts
1	**Montreal Canadiens**	60	34	16	10	189	138	78
2	Toronto Maple Leafs	60	31	19	10	209	172	72
3	Boston Bruins	60	26	23	11	190	175	63
4	Detroit Red Wings	60	22	27	11	190	193	55
5	New York Rangers	60	22	32	6	167	186	50
6	Chicago Black Hawks	60	19	37	4	193	274	42

Scoring Leaders:

	Player	Team	Goals	Assists	Points
1	**Max Bentley**	**Chicago Black Hawks**	29	43	72
2	Maurice Richard	Montreal Canadiens	45	26	71
3	Billy Taylor	Detroit Red Wings	17	46	63

Hart Trophy (Most Valuable Player): Maurice Richard - Montreal Canadiens
Vezina Trophy (Fewest Goals Allowed): Bill Durnan - Montreal Canadiens

STANLEY CUP

4 - 2

Toronto Maple Leafs   Montreal Canadiens

Series Summary:

	Date	Home Team	Result	Away Team
1	April 8	**Montreal Canadiens**	6-0	Toronto Maple Leafs
2	April 10	Montreal Canadiens	0-4	**Toronto Maple Leafs**
3	April 12	**Toronto Maple Leafs**	4-2	Montreal Canadiens
4	April 15	**Toronto Maple Leafs**	2-1	Montreal Canadiens
5	April 17	**Montreal Canadiens**	3-1	Toronto Maple Leafs
6	April 19	**Toronto Maple Leafs**	2-1	Montreal Canadiens

INDIANAPOLIS 500 - MAURI ROSE

Mauri Rose takes the 2nd of his 3 Indy 500's wins in a Lou Moore, Blue Crown Spark Plug Spl.

The 31st International 500-Mile Sweepstakes was held at Indianapolis Motor Speedway on Friday, May 30, 1947. Late in the race Lou Moore teammates Bill Holland and Mauri Rose were running 1st and 2nd. The pit crew displayed a confusing chalkboard sign with the letters "EZY" to Holland, presumably meaning for him to take the final laps at a reduced pace to safely make it to the finish. Mauri Rose ignored the board and charged to catch up to Holland. Holland believed he held a lap lead over Rose and allowed him to catch up. The two drivers waved as Rose passed Holland, with Holland believing it was nothing more than a congratulatory gesture. In reality the pass Rose made was for the lead and he led the final 8 laps to take the controversial victory. The race was marred by a 41st lap crash that claimed the life of Shorty Cantlon.

BOSTON MARATHON
YUN BOK SUH

The Boston Marathon is the oldest annual marathon in the world and dates back to 1897. Korean winner Yun Bok Suh ran the course in a World Record time (the only time a World Record has been set on the Boston Marathon course). Suh was also the race's first Asian champion and, at five feet one inch tall, the shortest Boston champion to date.

Race Result:

1. **Yun Bok Suh (KOR)**   2:25:39
2. Mikko Hietanen (FIN)   2:29:39
3. Theodore J. Vogel (USA)   2:30:10

BASKETBALL - BAA FINALS

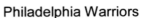

Philadelphia Warriors   **4 - 1**   Chicago Stags

The 1946-47 BAA season was the inaugural season of the Basketball Association of America. The league launched with 11 teams playing a 60-game schedule. The 1947 BAA Playoffs ended with the Philadelphia Warriors becoming the first BAA Champion beating the Chicago Stags 4 games to 1 in the Finals.

League Summary

Eastern Division:

		GP	W	L	GB
1	**Washington Capitols**	**60**	**49**	**11**	-
2	Philadelphia Warriors	60	35	25	14
3	New York Knicks	60	33	27	16
4	Providence Steamrollers	60	28	32	21
5	Boston Celtics	60	22	38	27
6	Toronto Huskies	60	22	38	27

Western Division:

		GP	W	L	GB
1	**Chicago Stags**	**61**	**39**	**22**	-
2	St. Louis Bombers	61	38	23	1
3	Cleveland Rebels	60	30	30	8.5
4	Detroit Falcons	60	20	40	18.5
5	Pittsburgh Ironmen	60	15	45	23.5

Statistics Leaders

Category	Player	Team	Stats
Points	Joe Fulks	Philadelphia Warriors	1,389
Assists	Ernie Calverley	Providence Steamrollers	202
FG%	Bob Feerick	Washington Capitols	.401
FT%	Fred Scolari	Washington Capitols	.811

In the 1948-49 season the BAA and National Basketball League merged to create the National Basketball Association (NBA). Today the NBA recognizes the three BAA seasons as part of its own history.

Tennis - U.S. National Championships

Mens Singles Champion - Jack Kramer - United States
Ladies Singles Champion - Louise Brough - United States

The 1947 U.S. National Championships (now known as the U.S. Open) took place on the outdoor grass courts at the West Side Tennis Club, Forest Hills in New York and ran from September 6-14. It was the 67th staging of the U.S. National Championships and the fourth Grand Slam tennis event of the year.

Men's Singles Final:

Country	Player	Set 1	Set 2	Set 3	Set 4	Set 5
United States	Jack Kramer	4	2	6	6	6
United States	Frank Parker	6	6	1	0	3

Women's Singles Final:

Country	Player	Set 1	Set 2	Set 3
United States	Louise Brough	8	4	6
United States	Margaret Osborne duPont	6	6	1

Men's Doubles Final:

Country	Players	Set 1	Set 2	Set 3
United States / United States	Jack Kramer / Ted Schroeder	6	7	6
United States / Australia	Bill Talbert / Bill Sidwell	4	5	3

Women's Doubles Final:

Country	Players	Set 1	Set 2	Set 3
United States / United States	Louise Brough / Margaret Osborne	5	6	7
United States / United States	Patricia Todd / Doris Hart	7	3	5

Mixed Doubles Final:

Country	Players	Set 1	Set 2
United States / Australia	Louise Brough / John Bromwich	6	6
United States / United States	Gussie Moran / Pancho Segura	3	1

THE COST OF LIVING

for pure refreshment!

COMPARISON CHART

	1947	1947 Price Today (Including Inflation)	2016
House	$12,400	$134,247	$281,800
Annual Income	$1,400	$15,157	$48,187
Car	$1,800	$19,487	$33,560
Gallon of Gasoline	24¢	$2.60	$2.68
Gallon of Milk	28¢	$3.03	$3.86
DC Comic Book	10¢	$1.08	$3.99

GROCERIES

Mrs Wrights Bread Loaf (24oz)	14¢
Fresh Creamery Butter (per lb)	79¢
Fresh Country Eggs (per dozen)	39¢
Airway Coffee (1lb pkg.)	38¢
Hershey Cocoa (½lb can)	15¢
Pepsi Cola (12oz bottle)	5¢
Imperial Pure Cane Sugar (10lbs)	98¢
Carnation Milk (6x small)	41¢
Jane Parker Sugared Donuts (per dozen)	24¢
Kraft's Velveeta Cheese (2lb pkg.)	99¢
Superior Spaghetti (16oz jar)	15¢
Campbell's Chicken Soup (No.1 can)	15¢
Del Monte Ketchup (14oz bottle)	25¢
Lady Betty Mince Meat (15oz jar)	27¢
Griffin's Peanut Butter (1lb jar)	27¢
Apples (each)	5¢
Texas Valencia Oranges (per lb)	6¢
Sunkist Lemons (large, per dozen)	30¢
California Iceberg Lettuce (per lb)	10¢
Red Potatoes (5lb)	21¢
Cauliflower (per lb)	12¢
Fresh Black-eyed Peas (No.2 can)	14¢
Carrots (per bunch)	5¢
White Swan Corn (No.2 can)	20¢
Aged Grain Fed Sirloin Steak (per lb)	63¢
Eastern Standard Oysters (per lb)	64¢
Morrell Savory Pressed Ham (per lb)	69¢
Sliced Bacon (per lb)	59¢
Armour's Corned Beef Hash (1lb can)	33¢
Kremel Shampoo	39¢
Palmolive Soap (bath size)	18¢
Gillette Razor Blades	13¢
Johnson's Baby Oil	89¢
Kleenex (2 boxes)	29¢

CLOTHES

Women's Clothing

Corduroy Jacket	$6
Silk Scarf	$1.95
Romaine Rayon Crepe Dress	$8.99
Ballerina Skirt	$5.95
Gibson Full Sleeve Blouse	$5.95
Chenille Robe	$5
Pajamas	$3,49
Cotton Bloomers	59¢
Seamless Nylons (per pair)	$1

Men's Clothing

Alpagora Wool Fleece Coat	$35
Knox Silk Lined Hat	$7.50
Uxbridge Worsted Suit	$45
Sears White Shirt	$2.69
Botany Wrinkle Proof Tie	$1
Jayson Striped Pyjamas	$5
Hansen Pigskin Gloves	$6
Gold Bond Shoes	$6.95
Leather Slippers	$5
Rayon Socks	39¢
Manhattan White Handkerchiefs (each)	25¢

55

TOYS

Sears 'New 1947 Model' Bicycle	$43.95
Pla-Mor Scooter	$1.79
Penney's Kids Automobile	$13.75
Steel Wagon	$2.29
Adjustable Saddle Velocipedes	$7.90
12in Toy Dump Truck	$1.29
Official Size Boys Football	$1.98
Streamlined Fast Freight Electric Train	$13.95
86 Wood Logs	$1.49
Play Doctor Kit	98¢
21in Cry Baby Doll	$4.98
14in Chenille Doll	$1.95
Plastic Living Room Set Doll Furniture	98¢
Toy Electric Iron	$1.89
Archery Set	$1.15
Roller Skates (balloon type wheels)	$2.98
Boys & Girls Story Books	15¢
Xylophone	98¢
Ukelele	$1.19

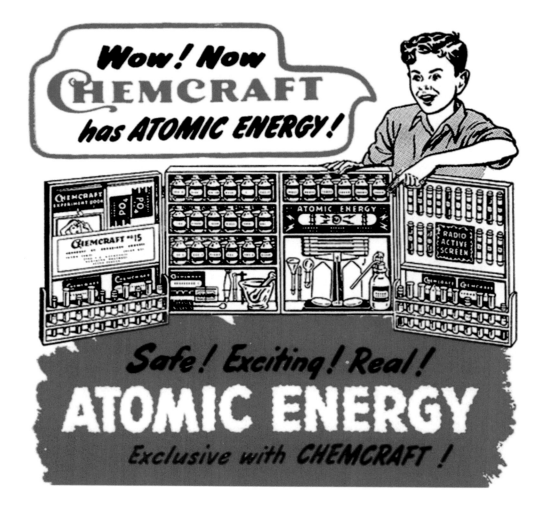

ELECTRICAL ITEMS

GE Electronic 10in Television, Radio & Phonograph	$750
Firestone Electric Range	$249.50
Truetone Radio-Phono Console	$129.50
Universal Vacuum Cleaner	$79.95
Electric Corn Popper	$7.90
Simmons Electronic Blanket	$44.50
Brewer's Electric Circulating Fan Heater	$12.50

OTHER ITEMS

Chevrolet Stylemaster 4 Door Sport Sedan	$1276
Goodyear Deluxe Tire	$14.40
Firestone Factory Method Tire Retreading	$7
Auto Batteries (24 month guarantee)	$11.65
Gas-Lined 20 Gallon Heater	$89.95
27in Wide Quality Wool Carpet (per yard)	$3
Craftsman Lawn Mower (16in cutting blade)	$21.95
Charcoal Picnic Grill	$8.97
26 Piece Stainless Tableware	$5.75
Indoor Clothes Dryer	75¢
Golf Bag	$2.97
Professional Plastic Curlers (deluxe kit)	$2

58

U.S. COINS

Official Circulated U.S. Coins		Years Produced
Half-Cent	½¢	1792 - 1857
Cent (Penny)	1¢	1793 - Present
2-Cent	2¢	1864 - 1873
3-Cent	3¢	1851 - 1889
Half-Dime	5¢	1792 - 1873
Five Cent Nickel	5¢	1866 - Present
Dime	10¢	1792 - Present
20-Cent	20¢	1875 - 1878
Quarter	25¢	1796 - Present
Half Dollar	50¢	1794 - Present
Dollar Coin	$1	1794 - Present
Quarter Eagle	$2.50	1792 - 1929
Three-Dollar Piece	$3	1854 - 1889
Four-Dollar Piece	$4	1879 - 1880
Half Eagle	$5	1795 – 1929
Commemorative Half Eagle	$5	1980 - Present
Silver Eagle	$1	1986 - Present
Gold Eagle	$5	1986 - Present
Platinum Eagle	$10 - $100	1997 - Present
Double Eagle (Gold)	$20	1849 - 1933
Half Union	$50	1915

Miles of wide, sandy beaches on bay and ocean. Intriguing rocky coves. San Diego's beaches are different.

Mingle with celebrities at Del Mar's seaside track. Racing Sundays at Caliente in Old Mexico, too!

Visit a foreign land, 30 minutes away. You'll want to see Tijuana, Old Mexico.

Deep Sea fishing deluxe, in sturdy, ocean going sportsmen's boats. It's only minutes from hotel to dock.

Cool summer days and nights in

SAN DIEGO

Here is a vacation you can stack up against any other... for sheer enjoyment...welcome change...new sights...new people ...even the thrill of a foreign land!

Head straight for San Diego, where California began. Enjoy the vacation variety of this gay city on a landlocked bay. You'll soon discover the simple charm which brings world travelers back again and again to revel in the never ending loveliness of San Diego.

That's right, dollar for dollar, a San Diego vacation will refresh you more...send you back with the feeling of having really been places and seen things!

San Diego CALIFORNIA CLUB

ATTACH THIS CHECK LIST TO YOUR LETTER

NOTE: Do not come to San Diego seeking employment. Please print name and address clearly on your letter.

1. I desire information covering:
   Vacation _____ Permanent home _____
   Business _____ Agriculture _____
2. Will start now _____ In 6 mos. _____
3. Send Hotel list _____ Auto Courts _____

Write **SAN DIEGO CALIFORNIA CLUB**
Room 8, 499 W. Broadway, San Diego 1, California

HOTEL ACCOMMODATIONS NOW. Consult your travel agent. His service costs you nothing. Often he can add immeasurably to the enjoyment of your trip.

THINGS TO DO AND SEE

★ Racing at Del Mar, August 5 to Sept. 20...at Caliente, Old Mexico every Sunday. ★ Daily harbor boat rides over 25 miles of landlocked bay. ★ Sports fishing boats on daily schedules. Reservations necessary. Nowhere else in California are harbor and fishing trips so convenient to hotel guests. ★ Old Missions to visit. ★ Starlight operas. Bring your camera and *bring wraps!* It's cool and enjoyable.

Spring's smartest styling...inside and out!

Made in the USA
San Bernardino, CA
14 November 2017